# Animal World

# Frogs

*Christine Butterworth and Donna Bailey*

STECK-VAUGHN
LIBRARY
A Division of Steck-Vaughn Company

Most frogs live in shady,
grassy places near water.
They spend a lot of time in the water.
Frogs need water to keep
their smooth, slimy skins damp.

Frogs have short bodies and large heads.
They cannot turn their heads around, so
they have eyes on top of their heads.
This helps a frog to see all around,
even when the rest of its body is
under the water.

Frogs have short front legs
with long fingers.
Their long back legs have webbed feet
which help them swim.

4

A frog does not run—it jumps.
Its strong back legs help the frog
jump a long way so it can
get away from its enemies.

This heron has seen a frog.
The heron is hoping to catch
the frog with its sharp beak.
The frog sees the heron and
jumps into the pond.

In the winter, frogs swim
to the bottom of the pond.
They hide in the mud all winter and
go to sleep.

In the spring, the frogs wake up.

They are hungry.

They swim up through the pond and
climb onto the bank.

They look for insects to eat.

8

This frog is sitting on a log.
It is waiting to catch an insect.
It finds a grub on the log.
The frog shoots out its long,
sticky tongue and picks up the grub.

In the spring, the frogs are ready to mate.
The male frogs sit at the edge
of the pond and croak to call
the females.

The females like the croaking.
They come to the males and mate
with them.
After mating, the females lay their eggs
in the shallow water at the edge of
the pond.

Each female lays over a thousand eggs.
The eggs float in a lump of jelly.
This is called frog spawn.
Can you see the frog spawn in our picture?

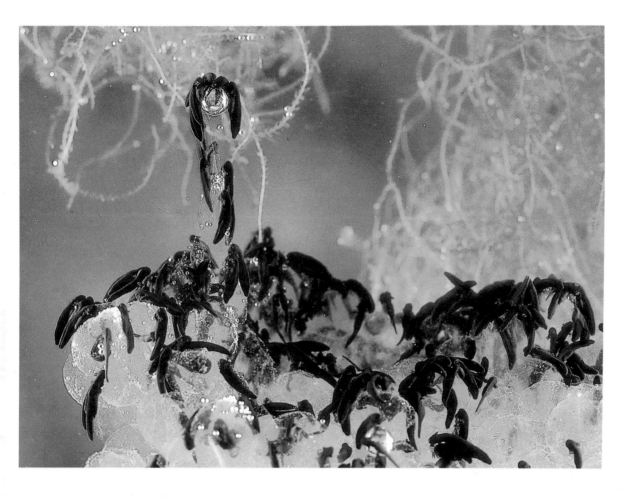

Two weeks later, the eggs hatch and
thousands of little tadpoles come out.
Many tadpoles are eaten by fish and birds.
Only a few will grow into frogs.

A tadpole takes three months to grow.
It stays in the water and breathes
through gills at the back of its head.
Its long tail helps it swim.

First the tadpole grows back legs.
Then it grows front legs.
Its mouth gets bigger.
Then the tadpole's gills disappear,
and it grows lungs.
Last of all, its tail disappears.

The baby frogs breathe air into their lungs.
Then they are ready to leave the water.
They must watch out for snakes
which like to eat frogs.
They will live near water all their lives.

Frogs live all over the world.
Not all frogs live near water.
Some live in hot deserts and
some can climb trees.
Most of them can croak loudly.
Some frogs and toads are very noisy!

Have you ever heard frogs or toads
croaking in the night?
You might hear some bullfrogs or some
male toads croaking to call the females.

Frogs have a pouch of skin
under their chins.
They fill this pouch with air
to make their croak sound louder.

The male bullfrog croaks to warn
other males to keep away from
his patch of ground.
He will fight another bullfrog who
comes onto his patch.

This Australian water-holding frog
lives in the desert.
It stores water inside its body.
The Aborigine people squeeze the frog
to get water to drink.

This is a poison arrow frog.
South American Indians use these frogs
to poison their arrows.
The bright colors on its skin
warn birds that the frog
is not good to eat.

Tree frogs are small and thin.
They have sticky pads on their long toes
to help them cling to trees.

Tree frogs can change the color of
their skins to hide from their enemies.
A tree frog has a green skin when
it sits on a leaf.
The skin changes to brown when
it sits on the bark of a tree.

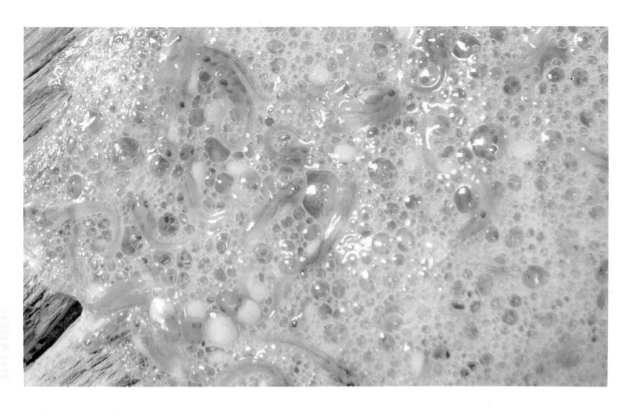

The female tree frog makes a frothy nest
for her eggs.
She beats the jelly around the eggs
into a froth.
The tadpoles grow in the middle
of the froth.

The male Darwin frog swallows
the eggs the female lays.
The tadpoles grow inside his body.
After two months, he opens his mouth and
out hop little, black baby frogs!

Toads look like frogs, but
they are often fatter.
Toads have short back legs, so they walk.
They do not jump like frogs.

A toad's skin is rough and dry and
has bumps all over it.
Toads spend most of their time on land.
They eat insects, slugs, and snails.

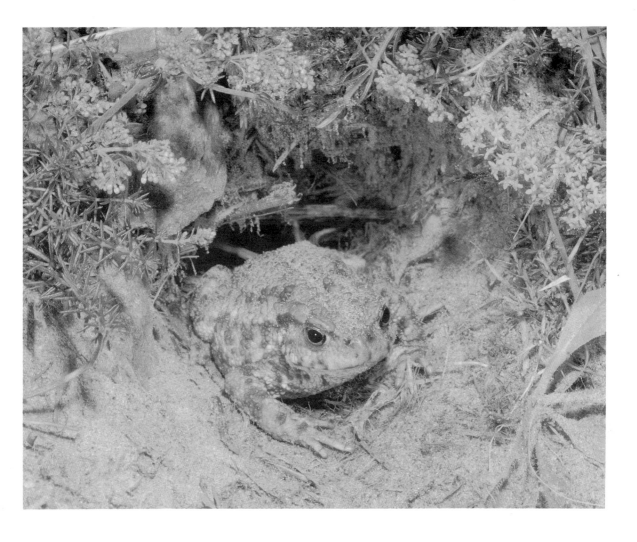

Toads live in holes in the ground.

They stay there to keep cool during the day.

At night they come out to catch their food.

This spadefoot toad lives in a hole
in the hot desert.
It digs the hole with its back foot.
This foot has a hard edge of skin like
a spade for digging.

The spadefoot toad stays underground
out of the sun until the rains come.
It can stay in the earth without food
for more than a year!

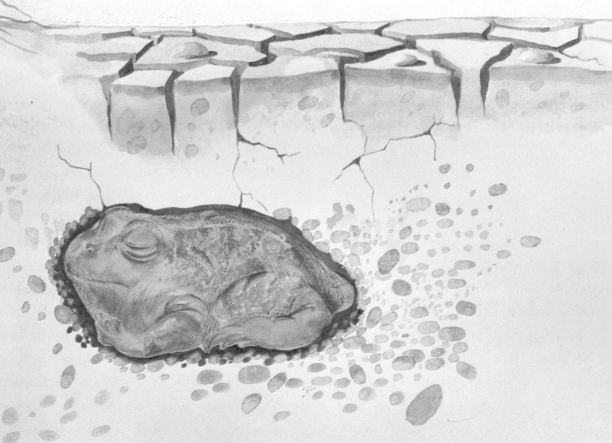

When it rains, the toad comes up
out of the ground.
It finds a puddle of water and
lays its eggs.
The tadpoles must grow into toads
very quickly, before the water
in the puddle dries up.

# Index

Reading Consultant: Diana Bentley
Editorial Consultant: Donna Bailey
Supervising Editor: Kathleen Fitzgibbon

Illustrated by Paula Chasty
Picture research by Suzanne Williams
Designed by Richard Garratt Design

Photographs
Cover: Bruce Coleman/Hans Reinhard
Bruce Coleman: title page (Roger Wilmshurst), 3 (Gordon Langsbury),
    4 10, 11, 25 and 28 (Jane Burton), 9 (Kim Taylor), 12 (Eric Crichton),
    20 (Leonard Lee Rue), 24 (Waina Cheng), 26 (M. P. L. Fogden),
    27 (A. J. Mobbs), 29 (John Markham)
Frank Lane Picture Agency: 2 (Martin B. Withers), 8 (Chris Newton), 18
NHPA: 13, 16 and 23 (Stephen Dalton), 19 (Anthony Bannister), 21 (S. Wilson),
    22 (James Carmichael)
OSF Picture Library: 5 (Stephen Dalton), 32 (David Cayless)
ZEFA: 17

*Library of Congress Cataloging-in-Publication Data:* Butterworth, Christine. Frogs/Christine Butterworth and Donna Bailey. p. cm.—(Animal world) SUMMARY: Discusses the characteristics of several frogs and of toads in general. ISBN 0-8114-2637-8 1. Frogs—Juvenile literature. [1. Frogs. 2. Toads.] I. Bailey, Donna. II. Title. III. Series: Animal world (Austin, Tex.) QL668.E2B87 1990 597.8—dc20 89-22014 CIP AC

1 2 3 4 5 6 7 8 9 LB 96 95 94 93 92 91 90